# I Did Not Cry for My Father

## THE IMPACT OF
## A FATHER'S DEATH ON A SON

BY

DAVID E. MULLEN, PhD

*the* Peppertree Press
Sarasota, Florida

ISBN: 978-1-61493-143-0

Library of Congress Number: 2012923978

Printed in the U.S.A.

Printed February 2013

# DEDICATION

*In loving memory of Father Jim Jones,*
*Whose wise spiritual direction and*
*compassionate heart provided a*
*gentle nudge to write this book.*

*And*

*In loving memory of Dr. Phil Quinn,*
*one of my closest friends—the older brother*
*that I never had*

*Two brothers in Christ who both died in 2011*
*Your special place in my heart and soul will*
*never die.*

*deep calls unto deep*

# GRATITUDES

We become who we are by our relationships and our responses to the events in our journey. This book is the result of friends and families whose lives have impacted me in important ways which are often immeasurable. They have gifted my life.

I am grateful for those persons who took the time to read the manuscript and offered suggestions for its development. The book is better because of their input. Of course, all errors are mine. Gratitudes to Sayers Brenner, Chip Conley, Cathy and Wayne Gonyea, Ed Carlson, Fred Gallo, Joe Bavonese, Grant Lowe, Janet Miller, Mickey Miller and David Thomas, whose feedback at various stages of the writing improved the overall thrust of the book. I am grateful to my brother, Doug, whose conversations were helpful. I appreciated the support and encouragement of my wife, Judy. Thanks to Marion Sandmeier, a wise, capable, and thoughtful editor, whose suggestions strengthened the style of the writing.

Thanks, too, to Valerie Knowlton, a former student and friend, whose senior thesis involved looking at my life through developmental theory. Her work helped me see my journey in a clearer way and provided added motivation for writing this book.

Gratitudes to the Tuesday morning men's group who completed the survey on the impact of a father's death on a son.

Appreciation to the following persons whose writings stimulated, challenged, and inspired my thinking about sons and fathers: Robert Bly, Sam Osherson, Neil Chethik, Alexander Levy, and William Pollack.

During my life journey, I have been blessed by mentors whose influence hopefully is honored through these pages: John Benton, John Evans, Sol Rosenberg and Tom West.

To Julie Ann Howell and Teri Lynn Franco, deep thanks to their shepherding process in the publishing of my book. They are the best!

David E. Mullen

# Table of Contents

*Father and Son*

# INTRODUCTION

*Death ends a life, but not a relationship,
which struggles on in the survivor's mind,
seeking some resolution which it may
never find.*

-- ROBERT ANDERSON, *I Never Sang for My Father*

H e lay there peacefully, a gentle smile on his face, wearing the blue shirt I had given him. Recorded funeral music softly filled the afternoon air. Garlands of flowers and wreaths to the left of the casket stood quietly like sentries standing guard. My sister requested that the wooden cross he had worn so faithfully be placed around his neck.

I had witnessed many viewings of the dead before, but this occasion was different. He was my father.

He had lived 92 years and 19 days. He lived much longer than any of my siblings thought he would. He had survived a punishing heart attack that nearly killed him and was also a prostate cancer survivor. My final physical goodbye was to kiss his cold forehead.

Dad's death has given me the impetus to write a story that I have been carrying around for many years. Life passages such as birth, marriage, divorce, birth of children, illnesses, and the death of loved ones are significant "marker events" in one's journey through life. They are the important threads that weave together the rich tapestry of a life.

This book is about the impact of my father's death on me, but it's more than that—it is the search to make some sense of my relationship with my father. Death often provides an occasion for this journey, if one is willing. Through the years, I have talked with other men about their relationships with their fathers. In my work as a psychotherapist, I have worked with many sons who have experienced father loss. I have come to believe that the search for the father is an important dynamic in becoming a man.

This book is one man's musings and reflections about this search. I hope that the journey that so deeply speaks to me will speak to other men and I invite them to reflect on their own search. Often what is most personal is most universal.

This is not a "how-to" book. There are plenty of self-improvement books at your local bookstore. How-to books appeal to us men, because we like to fix things— whether it's a child's bicycle or a broken relationship.

But there is nothing simple about fixing our grief over father loss. There is no one-size-fits-all healing method. A cookie-cutter approach glosses over the unique contours and shapes of our particular relationship to our fathers and the impact of their death on us.

The basic themes of this book can be stated in two sentences. The search for the father is universal for every man, whether we choose to recognize it or not. We grieve for the father we dreamed of, yearned for but never had and, hopefully, can come to the place where we accept the father we were given.

A particular audience of readers has guided the writing of this book:

- Men who want help and tools to understand father loss

- Adult sons who desire their relationship with their sons to be more satisfying than was the case with their fathers

- Wives, sweethearts and sisters who want to understand why the father/son relationship can often be so challenging and confusing

If this book achieves some of these purposes, I will be grateful.

This is a small book. It can be read in one sitting. What the book lacks in length, I hope it makes up for in depth. My hope is that you, my reader, will take unhurried time to read the book—allowing it to resonate with your experience and gently stir memories and evoke reflections. Like lingering over a satisfying meal or enjoying a good conversation, this book is meant to be inwardly digested and then hopefully dialogued with someone you care

about. We want to share what is important to us. It is
similar to the process we go through after seeing a good
movie. We want to talk about it. In the ensuing conversation, we often get new surprises, understandings and
insights through the interplay of questions, comments
and response.

This book is divided into four chapters. Chapter One,
"The Invisible Bond," provides a context and a starting point for responding to a father's death. As Robert
Anderson wrote, "The death of a father ends a life but
not a relationship." It is a relationship that continues to
haunt, comfort, intrigue, and irritate us sons all the rest
of our lives. Chapter Two, "Fathers and Sons," looks at
the push-pull relationships that often characterize father/
son interactions. Chapter Three, "How Men Grieve,"
focuses on the various ways men grieve and how men
deal with loss in a qualitatively different manner from
women. Chapter Four, "The Lessons of Grief," remind
us that grief is an important teacher. A main point here
is that how we handle our losses deeply impacts how we
live our lives.

The chapters to come discuss some important issues
men have with their fathers. They are necessary develop-
mentally for the son to separate himself from his father, to
own and express his particular strengths, and become his
own man. Some of the major challenges sons go through
are those of acceptance, authority and affiliation. Fathers
are the first men in our lives, and our first and strongest
vision of masculinity. Sons look to fathers for affirmation, for information, and as reliable allies in learning

to come to terms with mothers. As Harvard researcher, Sam Osherson, notes, "Our identities as men are often tied to a sense of shame, anger, or grief about what happened between our fathers and ourselves, and the way we confront opportunities as fathers, husbands, friends, and workers is often pegged to the relationship with this first man in our life."

This book weaves together my own truth with the truths of other men. How can it be otherwise? I invite you, my reader, to join in the unending journey of understanding one's relationship with a father who has died.

*My father, Edward F. Mullen*

# CHAPTER ONE

*The Invisible Bond: How a Son's Life Is
Shaped by the Relationship with His Father*

Edward Francis Mullen was born in 1917, the year
that the United States entered the war that President
Woodrow Wilson declared would end all wars and make
the world safe for democracy. My father was the oldest
of three children. His father, Edward F. Mullen, was a
butcher in Omaha, Nebraska, working with his four
brothers in a family-owned business. On the side, he was
an amateur boxer, Nebraska's heavyweight champion. In
my father's later years, he would proudly tell me that his
father would spar with the then-heavyweight champion
of the world, Jack Dempsey. He especially enjoyed telling about the time when, riding home on a streetcar, two
men started fighting with his father. He got off at the
next stop with the two men in tow, resumed fighting and
knocked them both out!

Sadly, because my grandfather worked long hours
and spent his evenings at the local tavern drinking with
friends, he was not available to my father or his brother

and sister. The only time my father mentioned outings with his father were when he would take him on a Sunday afternoon drive. Upon arriving at their destination, Edward was instructed to wait in the car while my grandfather visited a prostitute. As to my grandfather's marriage, my father told of many loud and stormy fights between his father and mother. Once, in the midst of a yelling match, my grandmother threw hot oil on my grandfather.

On a cold wintry Nebraska night in 1933, my grandfather came home drunk as usual, long after the rest of the family had gone to bed. He went into the kitchen, turned on the gas stove and removed the switches so they could not be turned off. Then he stuck his head in the oven. It appears that he intended to kill not only himself but also the rest of the family.

My father, sleeping upstairs was awakened by the unmistakable smell of gas. He ran downstairs to the kitchen, where he found his father slumped on the floor near the oven. When my father saw that the oven switches had been removed, he raced down to the basement and turned off the gas supply at its source. Save for his quick thinking, the whole family would have perished.

Thus it happened that at 16, my father was forcibly thrust into adulthood. With his father's death, he became the family's principal wage earner. Although he had hoped to study illustration in his senior year of high school, he turned down a full scholarship to the Chicago Art Institute. Instead, to keep food on the family table, he went to work at various jobs exhibiting a strong work ethic, which he followed all his life.

My father's deep dislike for the Catholic Church began at this point. Having been raised a Catholic and having served as an altar boy, he was angry and shocked at the insensitivity of the local priest at a time of great need for the Mullen family. When the family asked for a Catholic burial for my grandfather, the priest told them that they couldn't bury someone in holy ground who took his own life. My father's response was, "You can take your goddamn church to hell!" This sad and hurtful event sparked his lifelong mistrust, dislike and disdain not only for the Catholic Church, but also for all institutionalized religion. Retelling this story until he died, his pain and anger never left him.

Another significant event that I believe shaped my father occurred at the viewing of his father's body at the funeral home. In later years he would relate, "At the funeral home, I placed my hand on his cold forehead and vowed no one would ever control me." He strongly believed that his grandmother and older brothers had unduly controlled and put pressure on his father to work in the family butcher shop, rather than pursue a promising career in art. His artistic ability was unquestioned. At one point, Grandfather had designed the sets for a local theatre in Omaha. In that funeral home, my father then and there decided no one would tell him what to do. This was a transformative life decision. The theme of "no one will control me" ran swift and deep throughout his life.

A resourceful young man, my dad worked at a variety of jobs to support his family, including delivering groceries and selling door-to-door. At 19, he met my mother, Gretchen, in Omaha at a Congregational Church meeting for young adults. "She was one of the prettiest girls there," he later told me. They dated for a year. When his own family moved to Seattle to live with relatives, Gretchen took the train west to Seattle. They were married in 1937.

The Schultz family that Dad married into was a hardworking and very loving family—the family he'd never had. Grandfather Schultz came to the United States from Germany as an infant and worked as a federal meat inspector at one of the packinghouses in Omaha. He would often walk the long distance to work. For my father, the Schultz family was the warm, nurturing family he'd so desperately sought. When my parents married, they rented their first home from my grandparents for forty dollars a month.

I was born in September 1938, the first of three children. War clouds were looming large with Germany's invasion of Czechoslovakia. This was the year of "Kristallnacht," anti-Jewish riots in Germany and Austria. The Nazis arrested 300,000 Jews, 191 synagogues were destroyed, and 7,500 shops were looted. Germany's reign of terror was unleashing its fury, violence and cruelty, while an isolationist United States stood aloof and indifferent. Meanwhile, a beautiful British girl, Vivian Leigh, was taking her screen test for the role of Scarlet O'Hara in *Gone with the Wind*. It was also the year of Disney's first feature-length movie, *Snow White and the Seven Dwarfs*. Detroit's "Black Bomber," Joe Louis, knocked out

Germany's Max Schmeling in the first round at Yankee Stadium. Superman, the man of steel, first hit the newsstands in this year.

During the first six years of my life, I don't remember much about my relationship with my father. When I later asked him about some of the things we did, he talked of taking trips on the "El" (the elevated train) in Chicago on weekends and walking near Lake Michigan with my little finger in his hand. These are the few moments of tenderness that he described. I wish I could remember them.

It was around my eighth year that I began to notice conflict between my parents. My father was loud, bullish and foul-mouthed at times. Like gasoline poured on a fire, alcohol fueled his volatile behavior. By contrast, my mother was the appeaser, the placator. In the midst of his drunken tirades, she became silent and stoic. A woman of her generation, I don't think that she thought she could leave him and start over.

When I was a youngster, there were times my father would storm out of the house, threatening to leave us for good. I felt scared and wondered what would happen to us. Early on, I learned to appease him, just as my mother did. When he yelled, I would go silent. While he never hit me, his anger frightened me. As a result, anger was one of the most difficult emotions for me to deal with. I had trouble both expressing my anger and receiving the anger of others.

Particularly hurtful were my father's angry outbursts toward my mother in public. Often at family gatherings, such as weddings and funerals, he would become upset about something and begin to yell at my mother, his voice sharp and biting. I cannot ever remember his apologizing to her or anyone else for his verbal outbursts. I don't think he cared what anyone thought about his behavior. Whenever he let loose to my mother with one of these diatribes, I felt sad for her, but I didn't know how to get him to stop.

I do have some good memories of my father. He gave me an 8mm projector for Christmas when I was nine. The two of us built a movie theater in the basement and showed the neighborhood kids the comedies of Abbott and Costello, Laurel and Hardy and W.C. Fields. I remember helping him build a rock garden on the side of the house. We also built a soapbox racer together that rode in the Soapbox Derby. He took us kids to an air show at Offutt Air Base (now the Strategic Air Command located near Omaha) and fishing in a river running through the sand hills of western Nebraska.

But when his mood shifted, my world shifted with it. His idea of discipline was to be critical and withhold support. The words, "you slop ass..." still are etched in my memory, recalling times when he would come down hard on what he perceived as my lack of table manners. This is probably the reason that to this day, I consider myself to have excellent table manners.

Dad held many jobs, mostly in sales. Usually he was one of the top salesmen at any company he worked for. But for various reasons, he would get tired of the company, get into a conflict with the boss and then quit.

"Nobody is going to control me," continued to be his mantra for life. You might say that it controlled him. Because my father was such a successful salesman, he was always able to get another position. However, his frequent job changes meant many moves for the family. During my early teens, we moved a lot: from Omaha to Orlando to St. Petersburg to Tampa to Decatur, Illinois, and back again to Tampa in less than a year! I hated always being the new kid on the block. I attended six high schools in four years. In retrospect, such moves taught me to be flexible and resourceful. But at the time, it was painful and lonely.

I wanted a sense of security and emotional stability from my dad. Living with him was very difficult. His mercurial personality meant I never knew what would set him off. I wanted him to be gentle and kind and loving toward all of us. I erroneously believed that if I pleased him, I would not provoke him.

The years in high school were unremarkable regarding my relationship with my father. He was not around much. Due to his strong work ethic and desire to provide for the family, he would frequently travel. When he was working for a seed company, he would be gone two to three weeks at a time, selling seeds to large growers up and down the Eastern Seaboard. He sometimes would drive 2,000 to 3,000 miles a week—making eight to ten calls in a city and the surrounding towns and then driving much of that night to be ready for the next calls the following day. He often would say about those long, hard days, "I drove so much, I felt

I was part of the car." I missed interaction with him on those weekends he would be home. His "therapy" on those weekends would be spent in his greenhouses, growing beautiful African violets and gloxinias, instead of spending time with his family.

It was during those high school years I experienced some marker events. At 16, I came down with pneumonia and ran an exceedingly high temperature. I was delirious and thought I was going to die. During that experience, I remember praying that if God would spare my life, I would earnestly seek to discover what to do with my life.

The illness subsided and I began the search. The next two marker events were transformative. The first was seeing the movie, *A Man Called Peter*, the story of Peter Marshall, the chaplain to the United States Senate. After seeing the movie, I believed that God was calling me to become a minister. Like John Wesley at Aldersgate, I felt "my heart strangely warmed." The call to ministry as a profession was surprising to me, as I did not grow up in a religious home. I have described my father's disgust with the Catholic Church and disillusionment with organized religion. My mother was raised a nominal Lutheran, but her faith was more a stoic, rational approach. As a child, I had virtually no church experience.

The second event was attending a Billy Graham Crusade in the late 1950s. Culturally these were the times when mainline religion was very popular— Norman Vincent Peale was writing best sellers on positive thinking, Bishop Fulton Sheen was coming into millions of American homes weekly on television with his homey chats on living the Christian life and Rabbi Joshua Liebman wrote a *New York Times* best-seller entitled, *Peace of Mind*. Then there was Billy Graham, the charismatic Charlotte, North Carolina-born evangelist who began conducting his crusades throughout the United States and the world. *Time* magazine publisher, Henry Luce, financially supported and publicized his work and Graham became the leading spokesman for evangelical Christianity. He spoke to more people in the world than the first great Christian evangelist, the Apostle Paul. It was at one of his crusades that I stepped forward to make my decision for Christ as Lord.

I can still remember the experience after these many years. I felt that I was loved and acceptable to God even though I felt unacceptable to myself or to my father. God became for me the accepting, loving father that I so wanted my own father to be. With my father, I felt I was never good enough. I did not measure up. Later in college, I came across a book of sermons by the Protestant theologian, Paul Tillich, which further reinforced that feeling of acceptance. He wrote a powerful sermon retelling the basic message of the Christian faith in eight simple words, "Simply accept the fact that you are accepted." I was finally beginning to accept myself.

I believed I was called to be a minister. My father did not say anything to me about my decision. Again, I wanted his approval, endorsement and good wishes, but instead I got nothing. His silence was painful. Not long after that decision to study for the ministry, I was a freshman attending a nearby college. I was befriended by a

Presbyterian minister. He mentored me and helped me get into a Presbyterian college. He later invited me to preach my first sermon at the Sunday evening service at his church. My mother and grandmother took the bus some eighty miles to hear this gangly young, inexperienced nineteen-year-old deliver his first sermon. My father did not come. His absence was hurtful—one of the very important events in my life, where I again learned I could not count on him to be there for me. He gave so very little to me. When I had three major ear surgeries, my mother and brother came to visit me in the hospital, but not my father.

Now, with age and softer eyes, I can see that he was probably incapable of giving a lot because of his wounds as a son. Then I took his absence as another rejection. *What's wrong with me?* I thought. *If only I tried a little harder to please him, maybe he would love me.*

The years in college and graduate school were filled with studies and also a search for the father I never had. I had mentors who were like fathers to me. In college, a psychology professor helped me find healing for the shame and guilt I felt when an older neighborhood boy sexually abused me at 13. This was the first time I had received any counseling. At the time it happened, my parents handled the situation by ignoring it. A kindly minister comforted and supported me when my world collapsed after the first deep love of my life, my high school sweetheart, who I was planning to marry, wrote me a "Dear John" letter. A seminary professor who had an alcoholic father made me part of his family.

As I left home for graduate school, the visits home become less frequent. As I got older, I could not understand why my mother would put up with my father's mercurial emotionality, his putting her down, his outbursts, which often occurred for no reason other than that he was not the center of attention. I remember a particular visit to their home in California. I became so angry with him, I told him to go to hell. Witnessing their disagreements, I saw how she would clam up and become icy cold. I urged my mother to leave him. My words to her fell on deaf ears. She stayed with him for 50 years until her death from colon and rectal cancer in 1987. As a child and as an adult, I had often hoped he would die first, so she could have some years of independence and true happiness. It was not to be.

After I married and started a family, we moved closer to where my parents lived. By this time, they had moved back to Florida. In retrospect, my move was probably an attempt to be closer to him and connect. However, it was very seldom that my parents came to visit us, even though we lived only twenty miles away. In those days, my mother did not drive. Whether they visited was entirely up to him. I would often drive up Saturday mornings to have breakfast with them. Mother would put on a big spread of egg salad, ham slices and biscuits. While mother and I talked, he would spend the time in his greenhouse, growing beautiful orchids and prize-winning geraniums. Again he chose to spend time with his plants, rather that with his family—in this case, me. This experience just reinforced the belief that he was not interested in me. Why did I keep going? I still clung to the hope that somehow he would be different.

When my mother died in 1987 after a long battle with cancer, the family dynamics radically changed. As in most families, Mom was the glue and switchboard of our family. She held the family together. I was very close to her and I took her death very hard. She was the rock of acceptance and nurturance that provided a haven for us three kids. After her death, I became clinically depressed. As a mental health professional, I knew the signs and symptoms of clinical depression—I knew them intellectually, that is. This depression was different. It was not my client—I was the one who was depressed. I felt waves and waves of heaviness come over me, the slightest everyday behaviors became major challenges: getting out of bed, deciding what to wear or eat. I would spend hours each day just staring into space. The depression was very heavy. I owe my first wife deep gratitude for getting me professional help.

Thanks to competent professional help, the depression lifted. I resumed the Saturday drives to my father's home, checking in on him and staying connected. A year after mother died, he had a massive heart attack. Remarkably he survived it. I would continue to visit him every Saturday. Why did I go? I have often asked myself the same question. My best answer is that my mother would have wanted me to and because I was still trying to connect.

A decade after my mother's death, my father married again, a woman twenty-eight years his junior. My brother and sister were strongly against the marriage. Realizing how lonely he was, I was more supportive of his getting married. I agreed to listen to their marriage vows. The new marriage had little effect on our relationship. I still had to take the initiative if I wanted contact. A few years into the marriage, it became more obvious to my brother that Dee (not her real name) had married him for his money. They'd take expensive vacations. She got him to buy a house for her son. She was credit-card crazy. Much of my father's life savings were spent paying off her excessive spending. It was an ironic twist of fate that he whose mantra was, "I am not ever going to let anyone control me," was controlled in one of the areas that hurt the most—his bank account. She wiped out most of his retirement savings.

During the time of his second marriage, I remarried. In the second year of my marriage, my stepson Eric died. This was a very painful event for us. Before my wife and I married, Eric had lived with me and I had become very fond of him. The night he died, he had gone partying with friends, drank a beer and took a toxic drug, which caused him to be brain-dead. He was literally dumped off at the emergency room of the county hospital. We got the 3 o'clock a.m. call—a telephone call every parent dreads. At the hospital, my wife had to make the gut-wrenching decision to take him off all life support systems. A few days later, the funeral was held in the church where we were married. It was filled to capacity with many of Eric's and our friends. My father, who knew Eric, did not attend the funeral. I was hurt for both my wife's sake and my own.

My father's marriage with the "credit card crazy card" wife lasted only a few years. Dad would not listen to our exhortations to get out of the marriage. It became increasingly obvious what she wanted from the relationship, but he would not listen to us. Finally he divorced her.

He moved to a very quiet independent community where he spent the last seven years of his life. He loved his little neighborhood: quiet, safe and peaceful. He often quipped that this was "God's waiting room," for the community was located between a hospital and a funeral home. He could tell you where the birds and squirrels would congregate to eat and he could point out the beautiful cloud formations he could see from his corner window.

Increasingly he did not want to leave his community. When he was physically able, we would have lunch in the dining hall. His mind continued to be sharp to the end, but his body wore out. He depended more and more on his walker. When he had trouble getting out of the car or a chair, he would often say, "Don't ever get old."

I began to get glimpses of a gentle side of him. He seemed to be interested in what I was doing. I also was becoming gentler with him. He knew that we three siblings, my brother, sister and I, were the only family he had left. I would try to see him every two weeks and talk with him on the phone weekly. Of course, there were the times when I would leave from a visit with him where he had been irritable or unfeeling—a reminder that basic personality traits don't change. I told myself I would see him just once a month, but of course I never did. I continued to visit frequently.

When we would be together, he would talk and repeat stories I had heard so often, for example, how he had saved his family from death in Omaha; how Mom's voice was the loveliest voice he ever heard; and how in his work as an advertising executive, he came in contact with many religious con men. His favorite description of these phonies went something like this, "You would shake hands with them and then you made sure you had all your fingers."

That last year before he died, he would tell me he wanted to die. He was tired and worn out with living. At 92, friends who were his age had all died, as well as his younger siblings. He increasingly became tied to his little community. He did not want to venture out. Often I offered to pick him up and have him spend the weekend with us (a round-trip of 112 miles), but he refused. He was withdrawing his emotional and physical energy from the outside world. He returned to us pictures we had given him. He was ready to die. Putting myself in his position, I could begin to understand why he wanted to pass on.

Nineteen days after his 92nd birthday, after a brief illness, he died. I received the news when I returned home one Wednesday night after teaching a college class. My brother was the messenger. I was sad, but no tears came. Unlike the buckets of tears I experienced when Mom died after a long, hard battle with cancer, I did not cry for my father. I did not have any deep wells of sorrow.

The next days were spent completing tasks, such as preparing for the funeral, writing the obituary, and getting a caterer for the reception. We three siblings decided to have a part in the service. Since I was the minister type, I would lead the service. My sister and brother both made remarks about his life. The service was held in the same church where we had Mom's funeral twenty-two years earlier. It was difficult to write my reflections for the service, as I wanted to celebrate his life as honestly as I could, but without glossing over the fact that many times he was very difficult to be around.

His death was the stimulus for the book you are reading. This is my second published book. In many ways, the first was easier to write. My first book, *Living Your Strengths*, was about a movement within psychology called positive psychology, which looks at people's strengths and abilities. It emphasizes the importance of qualities like optimism, hope, resilience, and gratitude. I believe positive psychology is a needed response to provide a balance to psychology and psychiatry's overemphasis on pathology and illness. The emphasis is on what's right about people, among many other things.

This book is much more personal and my hope is that it engages the fathers and sons who read it and serves as a way to get a conversation going about their relationship.

# A Note on the Father Loss Survey

As part of my research for this book, I sent out sixty surveys to men aged fifty and older. While this survey is not large enough to be statistically significant, it does offer some clues to how men cope and deal with the death of their fathers. The ages of the men ranged from 50 to 78. Some were retired, while others were working. They were recruited from two church men's groups and friends I have known for at least three decades, who live in different parts of the country.

I recognize that our memory is selective and does not fully represent what in fact happened, much like a picture describes what the photographer sees through the lens. Nevertheless, memories can still be significant. The feelings surrounding those memories impact us and live on in us long past the actual event. Who can forget where one was and the feelings experienced when one learned that he received a significant promotion, the girl of his dreams said yes to his marriage proposal, the birth of one's child, the last child leaves for college or the death of a parent?

In this survey, the most frequently-cited feelings men reported at the time of their father's death were sadness, relief, and anger—in that order. The relationship the son had with his father at the time of death helps to explain which emotions dominated. For those who had a loving relationship with their father, the following comment is typical, "Seven years have passed since

Dad's death, I miss him and find myself still thinking, I have to tell Dad about that." Another man comments, "I think of him at least weekly." A number of men had a conflicted and distant relationship at the time of their father's death. One man comments, "I have to say that although I was at that funeral, I do not remember a single thing about it. I do remember my oldest sister, Doris, trying to start a family conversation after the funeral about remembering the good things about Daddy, but no one had a word to say." He goes on to say, "It took me a long time and a lot of therapy, and many years of 12 Steps, to begin to see how my inability to let go of my resentments and anger and hatred of my father were actually so self-destructive, at the root of my episodes of depression, and how I might go about the constructive work of forgiving him..." Unfinished business, unresolved feelings in the relationship, and the father being an insignificant figure in the son's life all contributed to a difficult aftermath for the son.

I also was interested in discovering in what ways, if any, the death changed the son's view of himself and his father. As many researchers have pointed out, the death of a father is one of the marker events in a son's life. The survey inquires into this inner shift. How does the death affect the son's view of his own mortality? Does he ignore and deny or embrace and accept it? In what sense can a father's death be a means of transformation, a healing of old wounds, an "aha" experience? Does the death bring to the surface regrets, hurts and resentments? Can the death be a stimulus for seeing the father in a different

way, with softer eyes?" Of course, there is no uniform answer to these questions. Every son has his own particular
story with his father and how he dealt with his death.

Here are some snippets from sons' stories about changes in their feelings and lives since their father's death:

> "I get the most out of life, never knowing when
> my time will come."

> "I find myself acting a bit like him, saying things
> he would say. It's a little unnerving at time."

> "I see him more sympathetically as a child of his
> times, doing the best he could."

> "I find that what he taught me has steered me
> through life."

> "I admire him for his integrity and caring for
> people."

> "He led by doing and not so much by caring."

> "Since my father's death, I have become more
> sympathetic and appreciative of him.

Those who stated that their view of themselves and their
father had not changed made some of the following
comments:

> "I have very few memories of him."

> "I could never count on him emotionally; he was
> a womanizer and gambler."

> "I was never that close that I could talk to him

about emotional issues."

"As an adult, I never gave him a chance to be emotionally close."

Often mentioned in the survey were broken promises. The son hopes for a particular event or thing promised, only to have his hopes dashed. Fathers often forget that kept promises are important to the son, because they are one important way the son feels loved and valued. When promises are broken, the son feels he does not matter— intentionally or unintentionally. Fathers being flawed, imperfect people with the pressures of finances and jobs will do this. I can remember as a father promising my son I would take him to an out-of-town professional football game. For some reason, I did not do it. For the longest time, my son held this against me. My word did not carry a lot of weight with him. I repeated with my son what my father had done to me. In my relationship with my father, I recalled things he told me we would do. We did not do them. I too was hurt and angry and took this as the fact that I was not important enough for him to keep the promise.

When asked what sons received from their father, the most frequent answers were work ethic, a model of masculinity and a model of resiliency. A strong work ethic is not surprising, given the fact that one of the traditional roles of fathers is to prepare their children to make it in the world of work and be successful. The way the father expresses his masculinity is one of the early models for the son to incorporate or repudiate. While the young son does not consciously realize the impact of his father's sense of being a male, through his father's actions (such as, the way he treats his mother, handles finances, deals with stress, or handles conflicts and differences) the son learns a lot by observation. As Eliza Doolittle told Professor Henry Higgins in *My Fair Lady*, "Don't tell me you love me, show me!" As Stanford psychologist, Albert Bandura, and others have noted in their research, observation is a powerful way of learning.

Many in the father loss survey mentioned that resiliency was an important gift their fathers gave them. Simply put, resiliency is the ability to bounce back when life throws a curve ball, to bring some good out of an adversity. You have to take risks, although there are no guarantees. Again, observation is the key. It is by the son observing how the father deals with setbacks, failures, and unforeseen emergencies or obstacles that gives the son an important model for resilience.

In my situation, one of my father's great strengths was resiliency. Beginning at 16 when he turned off the gas burners to save his family from a certain death and throughout his life, he modeled resiliency. I never heard him complain very much when he lost a job or a business deal did not work out. He just kept "beating the bushes" (his favorite phrase for looking for new clients and business). Knocked down, he would pick himself up and keep going. Many times in my life when faced with adversity or extremely challenging situations and I would be tempted to give up and throw in the towel, I would think of my father's resiliency. That model has served me well. It spurred me on. It is one of his most important gifts to me.

For example, in my early thirties I was an associate pastor of a suburban church in Florida. I had conflicts with the senior pastor. His style of ministry was very different from mine and I was much younger. I was not having much success resolving our differences. It got to the point where we both did our jobs, but hardly talked to each other. Despite my efforts to get him to agree to outside consultation to resolve our differences, he refused. Shortly thereafter, at the monthly board meeting, he brought up our conflict and said that he believed that it was God's will that we both not continue to work together. Of course, I was the one who was let go. In retrospect, it was quite a power play. The upshot was I did not have a job and agonized over what to do. During the time of decision-making following that event, I had breakfast with my dad and expressed my situation. I discussed my options and my anxieties. He listened very attentively, which was rare for him and then said something I have never forgotten over all these years, "…you have to take risks, even though there are no guarantees."

# CHAPTER TWO:

## *Father and Son Relationships, The Push and Pull*

### SONG FOR MY FATHER

*(Words mostly by Woody Guthrie)*

(Refrain)
In my heart I hear you sing again
Every note as natural as then
And when I sing this song
For family and friends

In my heart I hear your voice again.
I know your troubled times took many years away
And pain and sorrow with you every day
But deep within your heart of hunger
There were always melodies
Passed from you to me.

(Refrain)

It's been a long, long time ago
Since my father's songs were heard
But the child I can't outrun
still hangs on every word.

(Refrain)

What a blessing it would be, if all sons were able to sing this wonderful Woody Guthrie song with such an uncomplicated lack of ambivalence about their relationships with, and their memories of, their fathers.

Like all significant relationships, the father-son relationship can be viewed on a continuum. Unlike my generation, young fathers today are taking a different approach to their parental role. More about this in the concluding chapter. Mixed feelings often describe the relationships that we are most invested in. Hence, the title of this chapter: the inevitable push/pull of the father and son relationship. The dance many sons do with with fathers involves both wanting connection and not wanting it.

In the popular press, much has been written on the relationships between daughters and mothers and between sons and mothers. By contrast, relatively little has been written on the relationships between fathers and sons. For many adult sons, the father is the forgotten parent, the one who has remained in the twilight. This marginalization of father and downplaying his contribution to the son's growth and development has been perpetuated by outdated views of the roles of mother and father in family life.

One traditional view is that the mother provides unconditional acceptance, love and nurturing for the son, while the father represents the world outside the home, the world of hard work, achievement, competition and conflict. The father prepares the son to survive in that larger world, with skills that helped him make it. By example primarily, the father models toughness, self-reliance, use of the community, curiosity and exploration, proactive behavior and so on. The father's job is to prepare the son for making a transition to the larger world outside the family. For the son, the emphasis is on strength, control and rationality.

Interactions between fathers and sons are different from those between mothers and sons. Fathers emphasize *success* and what a boy does—not what a boy *is*—rarely, who a boy is with others and almost never, who a boy is mutually with others. The emphasis is on doing. The outward life of the son and his impact on the outer world is what matters. What's missing is an equally important validation of the son's tender and receptive side.

Other than expressing anger, most sons are uncomfortable with experiencing other feelings, for example, joy, sadness, disgust, or gratitude. They have difficulty naming these feelings and giving them a voice. In most instances, it is safer to tell someone you are angry with them, than to express that you are hurt by what they did. Feeling vulnerable is scary for men, because it means loss of control and the possible loss of oneself. Add to this mix, a relationship with a father who has not been emotionally satisfying and you have the recipe for a son's walling himself off to attempts by the father to connect. I think this comes about because our fathers have difficulty identifying and expressing these feelings.

Father love often is expressed in conditional terms, as a way of encouraging a son's achievements. Statements such as, "I'm proud of you," and, "You are an achiever," can be powerful validations and motivators for the son's development.

What I believe is missing in this traditional view of father-son relationships is an acknowledgment of the son's need for tenderness and affection from his father. In part, these needs remain unfulfilled, because of the father's lopsided emphasis on achievement. But a more important reason for the son's unfulfilled needs may be his father's woundedness, which keeps the father from giving tender affection to his son. The father is emotionally wounded, because he has never received warmth from his own father. His well is empty. A father cannot give what he has not received.

At the core of the developing relationship between son and father is what various writers describe as father hunger or the wounded father. Writes Harvard psychologist, Sam Osherson, in his book, *Finding Our Fathers*, "The wounded father is the internal sense of masculinity that men carry around within them. It is an inner image of father that we experience as judgmental and angry or, depending on our relationship with father, as needy and vulnerable. When a man says he can't love his children because he wasn't loved well enough, it is the wounded father he is struggling with."

Many sons experience father hunger as a feeling of emptiness, a deep, unmet yearning to experience love and warmth from the father. Because the father is unable to meet the son's need for affirmation, love and connection, this deep yearning goes underground. Poet Robert Bly writes of his father, "I began to think of him not as someone who had deprived me of love or attention or companionship, but as someone who himself had been deprived by his mother or the culture. This process is still going on. Every time I see my father I have different and complicated feelings about how much of the deprivation I felt came willfully and how much came against his will; how much he was aware of and unaware of. I've begun to see him more as a man in a complicated situation."

In my own father's case, I try to imagine what he experienced when he found his father dead in that gas-filled kitchen on Omaha's northside on a bleak, wintry February night. My drunken grandfather came home from the bar to kill himself. Whatever tenderness or love my father previously had experienced from his father had to be capped, as he sprinted down the basement stairs to turn off the gas that would have sent his entire family to their deaths. He had to stuff those feelings, because now, suddenly at age 16, he was the man of the house. He had to let die some of his cherished dreams—accepting a scholarship to the Chicago Art Institute, because "putting bread on the table" was more important than putting paint on a canvas; severely curtailing his social life in high school because he was now the breadwinner of his family; and looking after his younger siblings, instead of living a relatively carefree life like many of his friends.

As a man, he had to bury his wounds; expressing sorrow was off-limits. Instead, he expressed anger and a feigned attitude of self-sufficiency, thereby hiding his inner neediness. In retrospect, I can understand how this major loss, the death of my grandfather, turned his world upside-down and contributed to my father's difficulty in expressing feelings of tenderness and love.

Of course, I did not understand this. Like many boys, I mistook my need for connection and intimacy with father for a weakness. I could not understand why my father did not love me. I felt shame about it. Something must be wrong with me. I was not lovable; I was inadequate. How could I prove that I was worthy of my father's acceptance and love? Much of my life as a child and young adult was focused on that goal, though I did not realize it at the time.

In my later relationships with older males as mentors, teachers and guides, I tried to get from them what I did not get from my father—acceptance and validation. In most cultures, these older men serve as surrogate fathers—for example, the young shepherd boy, David, had King Saul and Carl Jung was the "adopted son" of Freud. Teachers, coaches and guides play an important role in the son's journey toward adulthood. They become part of the son's internal map. In ancient cultures, boys had ritualized activities to mark their entrance into adulthood. In our culture, very few prescribed rituals exist.

Jungian author, James Hollis, reminds us that it was the role of tribal elders to pass on the wisdom of the ancestors, to inform the youth of the gods whom he was to serve and who stood by him. Men today have no grounding in any tribal or transcendent reality—such men are lost. They feel abandoned by history and the wise old men. They long for modeling and for the great teachings. They suffer their exile in silence or act out their grief disguised as rage. Such men are legion.

The Biblical writer had it right: "The sins of the fathers are visited upon the generations." The Old Testament writers who concluded that the Lord visited punishment for the sins of the fathers to succeeding generations (like in Exodus 34:7) seemed to have grasped a psychological reality, whether or not we accept the theology in that writing. The wounds transferred from father to son frequently are those of shame and grief. Both feel unimportant, discounted, devalued—worthless to each other as real people. Of course, the son does not understand this. All he knows is that his father is not around and, when he is, there is little emotional connection. What the son most yearns for seems utterly beyond reach: that he is his father's beloved son.

At age 16, when I had my religious experience of feeling accepted by God, God's acceptance of me became more important than my father's lack of acceptance. This was an important marker event in my life, a step in the process of healing my father loss. God's acceptance of me became the backdrop by which I sought to understand and eventually to accept the limited love my father could give me. Such self-acceptance is a process and not a single event. With self-acceptance comes the ability to accept others as they are. It took me over sixty years to accept the limited love my father offered. This process involved letting go of the baggage of false expectations, beliefs and hopes. It required seeing myself and my father realistically and living with that reality.

If a son is fortunate, he will later realize that his father is wounded. He cannot give what he does not have. The son hopefully recognizes that his father likely carried to his adulthood his own share of pain and loss. With his own aging and maturity, a son can realize the ways in which he let his father down and how his wounds kept him from being there for his father.

At a younger age, I could not see beneath my father's rantings and need to be right, a wounded person who needed validation, love and a deep listening to. Now I do see that. Then I saw his lack of emotional connection as a personal rejection, a commentary on my personal inadequacies. Now I know that he was incapable of deep connection. I feel a deep sadness as I write this, for I was a participant in this dance of come close/stay away.

In his book, *Absent Father, Lost Sons,* Garry Corneau writes, "…All men live more or less in a hereditary silence that has been passed down from generation to generation, a silence that denies any boy's need for recognition—or confirmation—from his father…"

Corneau goes on to describe some obstacles that keep fathers from being available to their sons. One is the traditional role of father as protector and provider. From the beginning, men have been scripted to these roles. Physically, men are stronger than women. They protect their mates and offspring from animal and human predators. As providers, our cavemen ancestors were the hunters, toolmakers, and berry and nut gatherers. They foraged land. Fathers took their sons "to work" with them and taught them the essential survival activities of hunting and making of tools and tracking of animals. These essential survival activities left little time for fathers to enjoy and delight in their sons, play games with them and get to know them.

Another, less acknowledged obstacle that keeps fathers distant from their sons is that in many families, mother and children bond together to exclude father. Father is the odd man out, the absentee adult who comes home from work for a visit, but lacks any real authority in his son's eyes.

In my work as a couple and family therapist, when I hear the mother say, "My children are everything," I make a mental note that there is probably significant marital distress. A mother's dissatisfaction with the marriage may cause her to invest all her care, attention, love and tenderness in her children, effectively shutting out the father in the process. One of the sons, usually the oldest, often becomes the mother's confidant and protector. The important and necessary boundaries between mother and son become blurred. This leads to the further erosion of the marriage and stymies the son's emotional growth.

In Pat Conroy's gripping novel, *The Great Santini*, we

see this scenario played out. The book is based in part on Conroy's conflicted relationship with his own father. The theme of the book (and later the film) is a classic one: the testy and sometimes tender relationship that many sons have with fathers. The father, 'Bull' Santini, an autocratic ex-Marine flight commander, treats his family like his command: rigid, demanding, controlling, and highly critical. He is physically abusive toward his older son, Ben. He expects his kids to be prettier, smarter, and above all, gutsier than other kids. For the Bull, winning is everything. Once, during a basketball game in which an opponent fouls his older son, Ben, Bull screams out, "You get that punk and put him on the deck. Get him or don't come home. It's an order."

In the movie, Bull attempts to make Ben "a man" by mocking his interests in literature and reading and his closeness to his mother. Despite his father's neglect and abuse, he continues to try to gain his recognition and approval. Eventually, Ben gives up the attempt and rebels against the model of a man that his father displays. In the process, he becomes even closer to his mother. He moves from extreme disgust with what his father represents to an over-identification with his mother.

When there is an over-identification with the mother, the son's masculine side becomes stunted. Comments Harvard research psychologist, Sam Osherson, "When a man feels too strongly the shameful and wonderful sense of being 'mama's son,' without a corresponding knowledge that he is also a 'papa's boy,' then his capacity for intimacy for both men and women suffer."

In addition to the primordial father-as-protector and the mother-and-children-against father complication, there is a third obstacle that keeps fathers from being available to their sons, an obstacle which centers around an important developmental issue. Sons often want to dethrone and undercut their fathers, but at the same time, they want to cuddle up and be close to them. In part, this is a restating of the classical Oedipal myth—the son wants to get rid of the old man, so he can have mother all to himself. Freud used this ancient Greek myth to explain how around ages four to six, boys break away from mother emotionally and begin to identify with father. In the process, they become competitive against the very father with whom they are beginning to identify. This is a necessary developmental task. What the Greek myth and Freud's restatement overlook is that the son wants the love and blessing of the father, in addition to wanting to throw the old man off the throne.

As the son grows up, he often feels needy, yearning for intimacy and connection with his father and other males. But at same time, he feels ashamed of this neediness, this yearning, this perceived weakness in his masculinity. Culture reinforces this. In the white Anglo-Saxon Protestant culture of which I am most aware, little validation is given to the son's need for his father's tenderness or for his need to connect with other males. It is a telling commentary that for heterosexual males, often the only culturally-sanctioned arenas for men giving and receiving affection from men are in sports and combat. In these limited settings, the cultural eyebrow is not raised when a male comforts a wounded comrade or when a football player pats another on the fanny.

Thus, sons often get a one-dimensional picture of what it means to be male. The messages they receive are many. Be tough. Compete. Ignore your pain and perform. Put aside imagination, tenderness and vulnerability. In Arthur Miller's play, *The Death of a Salesman*, Willy Loman exhorts his young sons on how to be successful. "The man who makes an appearance in the business world, the man who creates personal interest, is the man who gets ahead. Be liked and you will never want." (*Death of a Salesman*, Act 1). While the play was written in the fifties as an exploration of the American way to success, its message is still timely today. Many of us never learned that this message is limited. We did not learn the importance of failure and learning from it, that men can be tender as well as tough and that the size of one's bankroll is not the measure of a man. We did not see our fathers struggling with failure or admitting error. We did not see them accepting comfort in a difficult time—or, if we did, it seemed so extreme and disturbing as to be source of shame for us.

A father is a son's first role model. The son can rebel against it or integrate parts of it. If a father neglects his own emotional life, his son is likely to follow. A son's neglect of his emotional life has serious consequences, not only emotionally, but physically as well. Men who have been fed a diet of "no pain, no gain" and "winning is not the only thing, it's everything," grow up to be highly competitive, aggressive, take-charge guys who are often oblivious to their body's warning signals of heart attack, stroke, cancer, and other serious diseases. One patient told me after he had a heart attack, "I saw my body as a machine. I thought you could just fix it like a car when it breaks down." Women are much more in tune with the cries, alarms and seasons of their bodies than men. Unfortunately, there is a large disconnect between men and their bodies.

We men learn to disregard, deny or downplay our feelings from the very beginning. In a study of newborns in a large metropolitan hospital, the researchers were interested in discovering the amount of time nurses took to respond to the infants' cries. Researchers at a New York hospital found that the nurses responded more quickly to the baby girls' cries than their male counterparts. Starting in the crib, boys' cries are given less attention. Early on, then, we men learn that expressing feelings of distress, extreme discomfort or pain are not deemed important or worthy of a prompt response.

Like the father, the son, for all or some of the reasons stated above, learns to deny his inner life. He grows up not giving it the attention, credence and listening it deserves. This mutual disregard of emotion prevents sons and fathers from building an emotional connection. Both carry with them buckets of unspoken words and feelings that need to be shared—but aren't. For example, I always felt free to tell my father about my achievements and plans for the future. He would listen to this because he, too, valued achievement and working hard. But when it came to expressing my disappointments about our relationship—his lack of emotional support, my anger for the way he treated my mother, and my deep hurt and sadness that he would never say he was sorry—I was silent. Because of other experiences with him of not being listened to, I hid my emotional pain. I felt like an emotional coward.

Some sons do acknowledge and speak of their pain to their fathers—and they are heard. Sadly, these are in the minority. Many others get into fights, steal cars, get high on booze and drugs and sex, or drop out of school. Although they may not know it, these behaviors are often the only way they know how to get father's attention. Negative attention is better than no attention.

Thus, there is in most sons this yearning for closeness, acceptance, approval and blessing. Sadly, for many, it goes unexpressed and unshared. If we are fortunate and have a wife who really listens, or a good buddy, or a paid "listener"(therapist), we have an outlet. If not, we go the way of finding mentors—older men, who not only teach us their skills and pass on their experience, but who in essence assume the role of father for us. Although many would deny it, as one mentor flat out told me, "I am not going to be your father!"

The bottom line is that a father's death often brings to the surface the unexpressed longings for closeness, affection and connection the son so much desired; the hopes, regrets and appreciations that the son will never be able to offer the father; the opportunity to clear the air on things that mattered in the relationship and for them both to give and receive blessing.

It is no wonder that for many males, the death of the father is a powerful emotional event; to which we now turn.

# CHAPTER THREE:

## *How Men Grieve*

As the days go by,
I keep thinking,
"When does it end?
Where's the day I'll have
Started forgetting?"
But I just go on
Thinking and swearing
And cursing and crying
And turning and reaching
And waking and dying
And no,
Not a blessed day
But you're still somehow
A part of my life
And you won't go away.

—Stephen Sondheim

One of the inescapable facts of living is the experience of loss. We lose people who matter to us. Like a rolling stream, it (death) carries its' sons away. The

Buddha reminds us, "In this life we have ten thousand joys and ten thousand sorrows." Consider some of the losses we face through our journey in life: the loss of innocence, the loss of childhood as we move into adolescence and leaving home to make our way through the world. Most people are able to manage loss on their own. Humans have an innate resilience.

The death of a person close to us is one of the most significant losses we face. Every man will grieve at his own pace and should not worry about "being over it by now." My clinical work and research have confirmed that there is not one particular way men grieve. Men do not need to be told, shamed or pushed by well-meaning friends with expectations to "let it all hang out," "you're bottling up your grief," and so on. The experience of that loss depends on many factors: the nature of our relationship to the one who has died, the circumstances of the person's death, how we have experienced other important losses and the meaning we give to the death.

Alexander Levine reminds us that grief lasts a lifetime. It is up to us whether we close around the pain and it diminishes our life or we open to it to include not just our own pain but the pain we share with all sentient beings—a life huddled in the corner or a life exposed to love and healing.

We now know that there is no universal way to mourn the death of a loved one. In 1969, psychiatrist Elizabeth Kubler-Ross wrote the best-selling book, *On Death and Dying*. This book opened up a lively and important discussion of a subject that had been largely ignored until that time—caring for the dying. In the book, she outlined the various emotional stages that the dying individual goes through: shock and denial; resentment and guilt; and finally, bargaining, depression and acceptance. For many health professionals, these stages became the gold standard for working with the dying person and his or her family.

Much subsequent research and clinical work has demonstrated that there is not one particular way people grieve. Noted grief researcher, Robert Neimeyer, writes that scientific studies have failed to support a clear and orderly sequence of adaptation to loss or to identify any clear endpoint to grieving that would designate a state of recovery. For Niemeyer, finding a meaning in response to loss is the central process in grieving. Other studies show that those coping with loss effectively were those who alternated between "loss-oriented coping," which involves thinking about the loss and what it means for the person and "restoration-oriented coping," which involves planning for the future and problem solving.

The important point is that the death of a father has different meanings to each surviving child, based on his relationship with the parent and his own past losses. Even for siblings who are middle-aged or older, rivalry over parental favoritism can persist well after the death of the father.

# WAYS MEN GRIEVE

Every man will grieve at his own pace and should not worry about "being over it by now." We grieve as we live. If someone is a reserved stoic in life in general, that person is likely to grieve as a reserved stoic. If someone finds it easy to express emotion in life, then that person will be more likely to show grief by expressing emotion. What is important is that grief be expressed. What is not important is the specific manner in which that expression occurs.

Sigmund Freud was 40 when his father, Jacob, died. He called his father's death, "the most important event, and the most poignant loss in a man's life." He went on the say that "...the death of the old man affected me profoundly. I valued him highly, understood him very well, and with that combination of deep wisdom and romantic lightheartedness peculiar to him he had meant a great deal to me. His life had been over a long time before he died, but his death seemed to have aroused in me memories of all the early days. I now feel quite uprooted."

Freud's ability to articulate his feelings about his father's death is not common among men. Most men find it difficult to express their deepest feelings, especially feelings of vulnerability and sadness.

Beginning in childhood, most men are taught to be tough, take charge and not cry. A dear colleague and friend of mine, Joe Bavonese, shared a story when he was playing Little League baseball in the fourth grade. Joe struck out, went to the bench and cried. His coach yelled at him and said, "Baseball players (that is, men) don't cry." Commented Joe, "I worked really hard that entire season not to cry (unfortunately I struck out a lot that half-year!) and by the end of the year, I was proud to be able to strike out and 'take it like a man.'" It took him years of therapy to undo that, however.

Cultural images of men being independent, strong, and cool under pressure reinforces the message to avoid showing signs of vulnerability, sadness or dependence. There is some positive effect of this, too—to have men to be tough soldiers, fighters—competitors. It is all in the balance, not either-or. However, many men do not find talking about their grief a particularly safe thing to do.

Of course, many grieving men never find their way to a therapist's office. The fact is that most men are able to manage loss on their own. Humans have an innate resilience. Many of us are stronger than we realize.

However, some men won't seek support, even when they need it the most, and this inability is closely related to their need to be self-sufficient and not be vulnerable.

Having to ask for help or emotional support makes many males anxious and uncomfortable, writes grief researcher, Alan Wolfelt. He asks, "How many of us know men who will drive around lost for hours without asking for simple directions? "Actually, this analogy to grief works well—driving around lost, he searches for a destination, assuming no one can help him. Many men, lost in the turmoil of grief, refuse to ask for the guidance and support that might well lead them in the direction of healing.

They believe professional help is for women—not men. Instead, they stay busy, self-medicate with alcohol and drugs, and have gratuitous sex. Workaholism is often a way men try to run away from troubling, disturbing and painful feelings. Self-medicating with alcohol and drugs can temporarily numb the hurt and the pain. Gratuitous sex offers a temporary fix and a high. Men engage in such behaviors, I believe, to maintain the persona of the tough male who needs no one. They want to be the rock Paul Simon sings about. "A rock feels no hurt, it feels no pain." All these are misguided attempts to deny the loss, anger and pain. Eventually, the pain becomes too heavy to ignore. It shows itself through depression and anxiety.

Some men are "high-risk mourners." These are men who are isolated and have no support system. Unfortunately they don't find healthy ways to grieve in a way that works for them. As a concerned friend or family member, you may notice them being excessively silent, overly busy at work or with chores, explosively angry or misusing drugs or alcohol.

I am reminded of the 1972 Democratic convention, when Maine Senator Ed Muskie lost his party's nomination to South Dakota Senator George McGovern. Speaking before TV cameras, he lashed out at a newspaper publication for dishonest reports about his wife, Jane. As he did so, he started to weep in frustration and anger. Muskie was later to say of those few moments on camera, "That changed peoples' minds about me. They were looking for a strong, steady man, and here, I was weak."

Many men come to feel shame for shedding tears or showing emotional distress before others. Thomas Golden, a specialist in male grieving, has found that men are less comfortable than women with dramatic release of emotion. In an interview, he commented that many men prefer to "slowly, deliberately chip away at their grief."

A major male response to grief is to exert control. From early on, men are taught to be fixers, to take charge, and to do something. Men are much more comfortable in taking action than expressing feelings. They are rewarded for their actions and achievements. The only feeling many men feel comfortable expressing is anger. The "soft" emotions like joy, delight, amazement, and sadness are considered off-limits. It is not a surprise that after the death of a significant other, many men feel they need to do something.

In research for his book, *Father Loss: How Sons of All Ages Come to Terms with the Deaths of Their Dads,* Neil Chethik surveyed 376 men about how they dealt with loss of their father. He found most men took action to deal with their loss.

He tells of a 33-year-old lobbyist who, upon hearing the news of his father's death, immediately exited his San Francisco apartment, walked to a cable stop and rode the trolley across town. It was something he'd done with his father when he was a kid. Another bereaved son, a 39-year-old lawyer, immediately sought solace at a donut store. It wasn't because he was hungry. "As a child, many Sunday mornings, my dad would get donuts to eat while drinking coffee and reading the paper," this man said.

When informed of his dad's passing on Sunday morning at 6 a.m., he immediately thought of getting donuts. About his response the son told Chethik, "I would say it was honoring his memory."

Another grief response men have to a father's death is silence. Notes psychologist Stephen Shapiro, "...silence is defensive, designed to protect men against being vulnerable to their own dependency needs. The silence proclaims the lie that men do not need others. And the lie undermines the mutual need that binds couples, families, friendships and communities." Regardless of the costs, most men simply clam up about their father's death. That's why efforts to get men "to open up" about their loss, whether in group or individual therapy, usually do not work.

The bottom line is that we men do not like to show vulnerability. Losing control of one's emotions is something men go to great lengths to avoid, especially around others. When I was twelve, I had my first experience of loss with the death of my maternal grandfather. I can still vividly recall that cold wintry January morning when my father woke up my brother, sister and me and told us about his death. The announcement was delivered in a matter-of-fact way. He simply said, "Your grandfather has died." My father expressed no tears, no sadness, even though the relationship between him and my grandfather had been a good one. They got along well and enjoyed each other. My grandparents had bought our first house in Omaha and had helped us financially when things were tough. I believe that my grandparents were the family he always wanted.

In a powerful way, my father modeled for my brother and me how a man grieves. In retrospect, I cannot remember a single time when I saw my father cry—even at my mother's death and funeral. He did not even express anger at the cancer that ravaged her body and took from him the helpmate and business partner who helped him build a very successful mom-and-pop business. I think he carried a lot of bottled-up tears. He suffered in silence. He had no one to comfort him. He was alone with no one to put their arms around him and say, "It's OK to cry. It is OK to feel sad, to feel down. I'm here for you."

Like so many men, anger and aggression were much more acceptable than expressing the deeper and more painful feelings of loss, dependency, and vulnerability.

Perhaps the two most powerful responses men experience when they grieve the loss of a father are feelings of abandonment and feeling closer to death themselves. Whether experienced consciously or subconsciously, these feelings permeate our very cells and the sinews of our bones.

The death of a parent revives childhood fears of abandonment, the anguish of being little and left. This is not surprising. The parent-child bond is one of the longest ties of our life and is usually the deepest. It creates an attachment that endures well into old age. Robert Anderson was right, "Death ends a life but not a relationship."

The death of a parent is the great separation, the large abandonment. Throughout life we experience many large and small separations and losses. Loss is the thread that runs through each life. For example, think back to your first days of school. Most children experience some anxiety when their mother or father leaves them. The separation anxiety that the young child experiences at the temporary absence of the parent lays the groundwork for other significant separations during life's journey. Several important separations come to mind: going to college away from home, starting a job in a distant city, breaking up with one's first true love, getting married and leaving one's family of origin, being let go or fired from a job one really enjoyed, and, of course, experiencing the death of a parent.

The loss of the surviving parent reawakens this primal fear of abandonment. It reminds us that we are truly on our own. Keith lost both of his parents over a period of eight days. "You are never prepared for the feeling of suddenly being alone—powerless—an orphan, no matter how old you are. It makes you feel like you have to grow up; you have to be an adult now. You have to rely on yourself, because they aren't there anymore." One son puts it this way, "Now I have no home to go to and no home to run away from." Gene Wolfe once said that being an only child whose parents are dead is like being the sole survivor of drowned Atlantis. William Gibson picks up on this in his little book, *Distrust That Particular Flavor*, when he describes how he turned to writing science fiction when the death of both his parents chopped his life in two.

Peter Grimsdale, a British thriller writer, describes how a parental death causes a seismic shift in the foundations of the grown child's world. "Suddenly there was no older generation. Even though I was in my thirties (when his father died) it was like being on a flight somewhere and going to the flight deck and finding no one at the controls."

Perhaps, most important, the death of the father reminds us of our own mortality, our journey toward death. With both parents gone, we no longer have a buffer between us and the awareness that we have no older generation. We *are* that generation. There is no intermediary between the grave and us.

For many men, the awareness of their mortality can be a freeing experience. It is an important reminder that we have to dance to our own inner drummer. We need to invest our time, resources and energy and commitments to people and purposes that matter.

Anthropologist Carlos Castenada, 70s author of the Don Juan best sellers, describes transforming meetings with the Mexican shaman, Don Juan. The books describe colorful and memorable teaching lessons with the shaman. I especially remember one lesson on death. Don Juan tells Carlos that he must so live as if death is always resting on his right shoulder. The point is clear: we can live our life most fully as we reflect on our dying.

The death of a father can be particularly difficult for sons who had a conflicted and distant relationship with the father. They may be upset and surprised over the extent of their grief. The surprise and distress is fueled by the growing realization that they will never be able to make peace with the relationship or to obtain the love, approval or recognition for which they had always hoped.

The comic playwright and director, Mike Nichols, lost his father who died at 44 of leukemia—Nichols was only 11. In an interview with *New York Times* columnist, Maureen Dowd, he commented how long after his father's death, of the many conversations he'd had with him. "I've had conversations with him about what I accomplished and what I didn't. I've had to be him and me, him proud of me. He was proud once when I won a horse show in boarding school. And he was proud when I was brave when I broke my arm. And man, I've hauled those out innumerable times."

Grief researcher, Debra Umberson, interviewed many people who had recently experienced the loss of a parent. She asks a son what he misses. He comments, "...I think one of the things I miss is not being able to hear him say that he was proud of me...I was always proud of him, but I never heard him say that. That won't happen."

Umberson: "Were you waiting for him to say it?"

Son: "Well, I guess more than I thought I was...About a year ago I was watching a TV show called *Major Dad* and Brian Keith was on the phone with the Major's father...one of the things the Major said to him was, "You never said that you were proud of me." And I was sitting there watching it. You know, tears were running down my face...I mean, I was a good kid."

Best-selling author on father loss, Neil Chethik, writes of the time when he and his father were going through his grandfather's possessions on the occasion of the death of the old man. Writes Chethik:

We kept at it until the glow of the afternoon sun had

waned. Then my father and I collapsed in my grandfather's heavily pillowed living-room chairs, glasses of the
old man's scotch in hand. We shared memories for a
while, then quiet. Finally, as the room faded into near-
total darkness, I heard a guttural groan. At first, I was
startled, and then I realized what was happening. I had
never before heard my father cry. I rose, and knelt by his
side. After a couple of minutes, he spoke. "I am crying
not only for my father, but for me," he said. "His death
means I'll never hear the words I've always wanted to
hear from him: that he was proud of me, proud of the
family I'd raised and the life I've lived."

The death of a father deprives many sons of the blessing they so much wanted from their father.

In my work as a psychotherapist, I've worked with sons
who have experienced the loss of a father. Initially, they
come usually because of a wife or girlfriend's insistence.
Seldom do they come of their own accord. "Therapy is
for women, not men." They bring with them unfinished
grief surrounding that loss, which can take many forms—
still craving the love and affirmation that they so wanted,
carrying a baggage full of anger at themselves and their
father because they were never able to express it directly,
and deep hurt and disappointment that they could not
count on their father to be there for them.

What do you say to them? I tell them to give themselves time to grieve; watch out for harmful behaviors
(aggressive behaviors, excessive alcohol and substance
abuse); and call in their men friends who have had a
similar loss.

I help them by listening to their pain and validating their loss. Where appropriate, I share with them some of my struggles with my father. It is a responsibility and a sacred privilege I highly value. In an important sense, I become in a limited sense a "father" to them.

In a different context, let me tell you about my "second son," Say. In the seventies, he came to this country from Laos with literally just the clothes on his back. Through much hard work, sacrifice and perseverance, he and his family built two successful restaurants in our town. I first came to know him through eating in the restaurant. We took an instant liking to each other. When the restaurant was not busy, he would sit down at my table and we would talk. I learned that he was abandoned by his biological father in Laos and raised by a stepfather to whom he was not very close. As our friendship grew and our lives intersected more, he invited me to various ceremonies where he was awarded belts in Karate. He had dinner with us at my home. I saw him get married, become the proud father of two boys and enter a second career. Often he would call me, "Papa," and I would call him, "son." I consider my relationship with Say very precious and I am honored to be called, "Papa." The point of this example is to say there are numerous opportunities for us men who have had difficult father relationships to be a father to a "son" who needs what we can offer.

Carl Jung observed that the greatest burden the child must bear is the unlived life of the parent. Each father's son must examine, without the motive to judge, where his father's wounds were passed on to him. James Hollis reminds us of some of the questions each father's son must ask: "What were my father's wounds? What were his sacrifices, if any, for me and others? What were his hopes, his dreams? Did he have emotional permission to live his life? What was my father's unlived life, and am I living it out, somehow, for him?" These questions are important. When we ask them, even of a deceased father, we are more likely to avoid idealizing or devaluing him. He becomes more a man like us, as a brother who has suffered the same ordeal.

Healing sons of father loss occurs on different levels. It is cognitive: dealing with the irrational ideas, the unvoiced expectations, and ideas and thoughts the son tells himself, for example, "There's something wrong with me that my father does not love me." It is emotional: accepting and embracing the sadness, anger, disgust and regret for what could never be. It is behavioral: getting the son to create a meaningful ritual, such as visiting the father's grave or journaling about some of the peaks and valleys of the relationship.

All this is challenging, important and sacred work. We need to heal some of our wounds with our fathers so that we do not let them get in the way of developing a "good enough" connection with our son or other men. We will discuss ways in which men *do* heal in Chapter 4.

# CHAPTER FOUR

## *Lessons of Grief*

*Whatever the nature of the bond, parents never leave us. After death, they simply move their residence from the outer world to the inner and accompany us for the rest of our lives.*

— Author unknown

One of the themes of this book is that a son grieves the loss of his father in his own way. Some sons experience the death of a father in gut-wrenching ways; others in quiet, often undemonstrable ways. Still others grieve over a long, extended time. Grief is multi-faceted and resists being put into neat stages.

The same can be said of the lessons we learn from father loss. One size does not fit all. Nonetheless, I believe it is worth asking: what can the loss of our fathers teach us? In what ways can it be transformative? What are some tools that other men have found helpful to do the work of grief?

The following lessons are gleaned from clinical inter-
views, research and my clinical and personal experience.
I will start with some of the universal lessons of loss and
move to the more particular impact of a father's death
on a son. My intention is to describe what I have learned
and hope it will invite other men to reflect on their own
experience.

---

## LESSON 1: *Grief teaches us that separation and loss are woven into the fabric of life.*

---

From the moment we are born, we are on a journey toward death. In life, few things last—whether institutions,
countries, or individuals. The reality of impermanence
serves to remind us that relationships matter. With the
finite time each person has, impermanence can nudge us
to invest our energy and attention in those people who
deeply matter to us.

Remember when you were a youngster and could
hardly wait until your next birthday, Christmas, or sum-
mer vacation? Then you got older, and you began to focus on when you'd get your driver's license (freedom!),
and then when you'd graduate from high school or college. Maybe you said to yourself, I will really be set once
I get married, land that dream job, and buy that house
with a pool in the suburbs.

Then, some years later, in our thirties or forties, many
of us recognize that we were not going to realize all these
dreams. Or, we recognize that the external trappings of
success, however our particular culture defines it, do

not bring us the inner contentment and satisfaction we thought it would. Sometime during those years, many men experience what Carl Jung wrote about: a gnawing inner discontent and search for something more. Jung uses the analogy of mountain climbing to make his point. He says that we spend the first half of our lives climbing up the mountain, our attention fixed on externals—money, possessions, and so forth. Then, around 35 or 40, we start climbing down the mountain. For many, the important focus moves from outward to inward. Not only do we become aware that we won't realize some of our dreams, but we also become aware of our mortality and limitations.

With an inward focus, some men become more introspective, reflective and spiritual. Loss contributes to this. Parents die. Relationships break up. Children leave home. Each of us has our own litany of loss. We are hit with the sobering reality that haunts us and will not let us go—nothing lasts.

Other men turn a deaf ear to these hauntings. They continue to lose themselves in their work. After all, is not that how society defines a man? His value, identity and worth are tied up in what he does. This explains why retirement is difficult for many men and their wives. Other men may escape into other addictions, such as substance abuse or gratuitous sex. And some explore and experience the truth of their spiritual nature.

The reality of loss testifies to the fragility and impermanence of life. If we choose to learn from loss, we can invest our energy and love in the people who matter to us. The fact that our lives are limited means that they are important. What Pulitzer Prize-winning poet, Mary Oliver, calls our "wild and wonderful life" ought not to be squandered on things that are unimportant. The impermanence of life, which grief teaches, can enrich our lives and make them deeper and fuller. Oliver expresses this reality very powerfully in her poem, *In Blackwater Woods*:

> To live in this world
> you must be able
> to do three things:
> to love what is mortal;
> to hold it
> against your bones knowing
> your own life depends on it;
> and, when the time comes to let it go,
> to let it go.

## LESSON 2: *Grief teaches us that in life, our control is limited—at best.*

The myth of self-sufficiency is shattered by the deaths of those closest to us by and the growing sense of our own mortality. Death is teaches us that we are not the masters of our own fate nor the captains of our own souls. We are mortal and limited.

This then can be a disguised gift that the death of a father offers the son: the sobering awareness of what we can control and what we can't. As we discussed earlier, Ideally fathers teach sons to be self-reliant, confident, and active in their engagement with the world. We are taught to be fixers and problem-solvers. Certainly, these qualities are important. However, when this conditioning is excessive, men become ill-equipped for the boundary situations all persons face—the crises of suffering, meaninglessness and loss. These are situations in which—at best—we have little control.

Men suffer crises of mind and soul when their customary efforts prove ineffective. The affirmations we learned as sons ("Try a little harder." "Winning is not the only thing; it's everything." "If it's to be, it's up to me."), and the frequent inner pep talks we gave ourselves when faced with challenges now prove ineffectual. We hide our feelings of dependency, powerlessness and vulnerability with a fake bravado or a feigned self-sufficiency.

In response to his father's suicide, at age 16, my father made the decision that he would never again let anyone control him, when he put his hand on my grandfather's cold forehead in that Omaha funeral home long ago. This became his mantra, the pattern that drove him relentlessly throughout much of his life. It cost him jobs, ruptured relationships and kept at an arm's distance a son who wanted to be affirmed and loved.

Certainly control is important in our lives. However it needs to be balanced with vulnerability. The difficulty is that my father was and other men are so focused on control that it becomes an all-or-nothing solution. Such an exaggerated emphasis on control is more typical of a 16-year-old, who is usually not yet ready for the most powerful, integrated and paradoxical solutions to come in adulthood. Then, a man can embrace both ends of the dilemma. He is able to comprehend and practice what my friend Sayers Brenner calls "dis/control." In Kenny Rogers' song "The Gambler," he reminds us that we need to know "…when to hold 'em, know when to fold 'em."

These boundary situations offer an opportunity for growth. We can reach out to significant others and let them know we need them.

---

**LESSON 3:** *The death of a father can help a son see his father with "softer eyes."*

---

From birth to death, we carry an internalized image of our father. Countless images, feelings, and thoughts of his become part of us. Regardless of the nature of the bond, our father never leaves us. After death, he simply moves his residence from the outer world to the inner and accompanies us for the rest of our lives. In fact, some sons are shocked or surprised when a friend or relative points out us that a particular gesture, facial expression or behavior of ours is just like our father's. Our response, of course, depends upon how valued our relationship was with him.

In his book, *Father Loss,* Neil Chethik quotes a middle-aged lobbyist he interviewed: "Periodically, I became him. Like every time I pack the car to go on a camping trip, I suddenly realize I've become my father. I have these strong memories of my father so methodically packing the car to be sure the space has been efficiently used in the trunk. I'm just as anal about that as my father was—but I have a smaller trunk."

The death of our father can help us remove some of the blinders we used to view him with while he was alive. Writes Jeanne Safer, "By dying, one's parents free you to appreciate them so completely, with a kind of empathy that would have been impossible to sustain in their lifetime." For some sons, the death of a father can be a source of new and important information and surprises. I remember reading the *New York Times* bestseller, *Flags of Our Fathers,* the story of the five Marines whose raising of the American flag on Iwo Jima was one of the most powerful and well-known photographs of World War II. The author, James Bradley, recounts that after his father's death, he was in the attic going through some of his father's wartime letters sent to his wife. In them, young Bradley discovered to his great surprise that his father was one of the five flag raisers. This was a momentous discovery for him. Like many servicemen, his father had never told him of the event or his war experiences. His father like so many of the "greatest generation" about whom newsman Tom Brokaw interviewed and wrote kept these matters to themselves.

For many sons, the death of their fathers is a significant marker in how they view him and themselves. For some, it involves an inward revision of the relationship. Shortly before my own father's death, I was beginning to see him with softer eyes. In earlier chapters, I mentioned that I carried a lot of anger toward him for the way he treated my mother and me. The anger kept me from appreciating his basic strengths and accepting what love he could offer me. Unresolved anger builds walls between people. It blocked me from acknowledging the love he had for me and from accepting him as a flawed human being and finding out, therefore, that it was nothing personal. It was how my father was with everyone.

In some convoluted way, I thought that if I let go of the anger toward my father, I would somehow be disloyal to my mother. I would betray her memory. So I kept the anger going even after my mother died in the late 1980s. As with all unreleased resentments and grudges, it caused me a lot more harm, restlessness and grief than it did him. Holding onto resentments, grudges, and negative feelings toward another usually does. This is where Father Jim came in.

I was seeing Father Jim, a spiritual director and Franciscan priest some months before my father died. A major focus of our work together was his encouraging me to forgive my father and let go of the anger, hurt and resentment that I'd been carrying all these years. Ironically, Father Jim had helped me years ago when my mother died. I had been in deep grief over her death and unable to deal with the loss.

This time, I was seeing Father Jim not only for spiritual counsel in dealing with my father, but also with my son, Michael. I was having a hard time accepting what my son could give me—his needs for family connection and contact did not seem to be important. I deeply wanted our relationship to be different than mine had been with my father.

With Father Jim's help, I finally came to realize that as with my father, so with my son—I had to accept whatever he could give me. I could not change my son any more than I could change my father.

This was a hard lesson for someone like me, who believed he was totally responsible for the relationship and how it developed, someone who believed he could "fix" relationships and make them better. (Incidentally, this is the false belief that leads many of us to enter the helping professions.) Of course, to forgive and let go is not easy. I was torn between holding onto the heavy worn bag of resentments and letting them go.

Finally, through much inner work, talks with Father Jim and prayer, I began to see my father differently. I began to forgive him. The change was not obvious to me at first. My sister, Kathe, observed my changed view of my father before I did. One Saturday afternoon, we were having lunch with our father at the dining hall of the independent living facility where he lived. During our luncheon conversation, he made some remarks that in the past would have made me very angry. My anger, scowl or displeasure would be obvious to everyone around me. This time, however, I did not get hooked. I did not repeat my former behavior. Later, when Kathe and I were alone that afternoon, she mentioned the change she saw in me. *Aha,* I mused to myself, *something is happening within me.*

The book you're now reading also contributed to this change. It, too, has helped me to see my father with softer eyes. The softer eyes and the forgiveness—these are so central—a factor in realizing that our fathers raised us during their own young adulthood, when they could not have yet attained the deeper wisdom that comes later. We must learn to forgive their, and our, errors of youth. Wisdom develops slowly over an entire lifetime.

Initially, my intention in writing the book was to provide some help for sons who had a conflicted and difficult relationship with their fathers, using my relationship with my father as a starting point. Little did I realize that the book would change me. As I have tried to understand him and put myself in his shoes, I have come to a deeper appreciation and respect for the struggles he endured. Such a concerted effort has dissipated much of my anger.

# Suggestions for Dealing with Father Loss

One important suggestion for sons dealing with father loss is to tell or write a story about their fathers. I would encourage sons to make this a biography. Such a process can result in a changed position of the son in relation to father, enabling the son to gradually separate from father and sometimes to love him in a different way.

Writing or other artistic pursuits, such as painting, singing, dancing or acting are concrete ways to celebrate beloved memories or to avoid tormenting ones. The very process of doing this can be healing for a son. As one writer put it about a father's story: "You can't make sense of a story—their story—until it ends. Of course it goes on, but then it goes on in you."

Each significant loss involves a story. The story deserves to be told. By telling the story, you make it more real and you gain perspective. You gain witnesses, who help give weight and meaning to your experience. They help to validate your outlook and feelings. Most importantly, by telling or writing your story, you can help others. This is one of the major reasons why Alcoholic Anonymous has been so helpful in the recovery of alcoholics. It provides a forum where persons struggling with alcoholism can tell their story. You leave a legacy for others to remember, by which they can direct their own lives.

What author Deborah Umberson discovered about

writing her mother's story after her death applies to men as well:

> Whether our own effort produces a book, a letter, a diary, a painting, a poem, a photograph, a video, or a blog, the process of creating something makes thoughts comprehensible and feelings concrete. Investigating my relationship with my mother on paper helped me organize it, grasp it and profit from it. Reconsidering her was as exhilarating as it was excruciating and gave me more hope and insight than I have ever known.

---

**LESSON 4:** *The death of a father can motivate us to deepen and prize our relationships with our own sons.*

---

This is especially true for men who had difficult relationships with their fathers. We often vow to ourselves that our relationship with our sons is going to be somehow different. We want to spare our sons the emotional pain, the betrayals, the unavailability and the broken promises that we experienced. We want to be the kind of father that we wish our father had been to us. While this is an admirable intention and possible to an extent, we will inevitably let our sons down in some ways, as our fathers did us. We must learn forgiveness of ourselves, too.

Nevertheless, our disappointments, regrets, and unfulfilled longings with our fathers can prompt us to make some important changes in the way we relate to our sons.

I believe the key is awareness of our relationship with our father. I can remember as a father promising my son I would take him to an out-of-town professional football game. For some reason, I did not do it. For the longest time, my son held this against me. My word did not carry a lot of weight with him. I repeated with my son what my father had done to me. In my relationship with my father, I recalled things he told me we would do. We did not do them. I too was hurt and angry and took this as an indication that I was not important enough for him to keep the promise. If we are willing, a reflective and honest appraisal of our relationship with our father will help us appreciate his strengths and teachings, as well as his liabilities.

In an important sense, our story with our fathers provides some of the raw materials for adding to the story of the relationship with our sons. If we view that earlier story with clearer vision and softer eyes, we have the opportunity to write our story with our sons with some different emphasis, punctuation, and new beginnings and endings.

As fathers, we want to pass on to our sons the gifts our fathers gave us. As fathers, we want to give our sons what our fathers were not able to give us.

With my own son, Michael, I hope I have passed on to him my father's strong work ethic, a model of resilience and emotional courage. This is the way I honor and perpetuate his memory and legacy. Unlike my father, who would never admit he was wrong or sorry for the hurts he caused others, I try to model for my son a father who can admit he is sorry, acknowledge the ways I have let him down, and ask for forgiveness.

With time and with the eyes of forgiveness, we are able to more clearly and compassionately see our fathers as struggling human beings doing the best they could with their own limited resources. I have more compassion for what my father went through, his successes and failures, and the adversities he faced and triumphed over. I know I could not have experienced that if I remained stuck in my anger.

Acceptance and forgiveness are the invisible threads that bind us to our fathers, as well as to our sons. Forgiveness breaks open our hardened hearts to take them in and accept them. Hopefully, we can come to the place where we can acknowledge that they did their best with what they had.

Perhaps the most important gift we can give our sons is our affection and blessing. As the survey on father loss reported, what many men missed receiving from their father was affection, his participation in their life and the confidence that they could depend on him. Most sons want to deeply know: "He's there for me and I know he loves me."

To put it another way, most sons want a blessing from their father. From the Old Testament story of Jacob's wrestling with the angel at Peniel and refusing to let him go until he received a blessing, to the Gospel writer's account of the baptism of Jesus when God declares, "This is my beloved son in whom I am well pleased," blessing is vital to the son.

Author Neil Chethik describes the importance of receiving his father's blessing:

He'd said: "I want to tell you now how proud I am of you, of the choices you've made, of the life you've created." At the time, his father had just died, and my father was poignantly aware of having missed his dad's affirmation in his own life.

My father's blessing was especially important to me because I was concerned that I'd disappointed him. He'd put me through college, and now, five years into my career, I'd quit a good job with no plan for what I'd do next. When my father told me he was proud of the choices I'd made, I took it to mean that he supported me in my decision to stop and reevaluate my career direction. I felt the pressure lift and began to trust myself to make the right next step.

One of the men in the survey on father loss described how he tried to connect with his son: "I initiated a lot of conversation with my 20-year-old son about my troubled relationship with my father, in order to start over as a father. I bought each of us a copy of a book about father/son relationship. Went through a chapter each week and discussed it in terms of our relationship...invited him to confront me with any personal issue or complaints he had with the way I had failed him as a child growing up...he did open up honestly with me somewhat. That was a very positive thing that happened."

In conclusion, father loss offers us sons great pain and great opportunity. My hope is that this book has given you some tools to appreciate who your father has been to

you and recognize the ways he has failed you. We are the
son, as Wallace Stevens reminds us:

...*who bears upon his back*

The father that he loves, and bears him from

The ruins of the past, out of nothing left,

In my opinion, all important relationships if they are
to be authentic need to include this mix of heartfelt appreciation and some deep regret and lots of joy. I like
the way Sam Osherson puts it—we need to "...retrieve
a firm, sturdy appreciation of the heroism and failure in
our fathers' lives."

In doing this, we receive our father's blessing, make it
our own, and pass it on. In this way, we honor our fathers
and ourselves.

# REFERENCES

Chetkik, Neil. *Father Loss: How Sons of All Ages Come to Terms with the Deaths of Their Dads*. New York: Hyperion, 2000.

Corneau, Garry. *Absent fathers, Lost Sons*. Boston: Shambala, 1991.

Golden, Thomas and Miller, James. *When a Man Faces Grief*. Fort Wayne, IN: Willowgreen Publishers, 1998.

Hollis, James. *Under Saturn's Shadow: the Wounding and Healing of Men*. Toronto: Inner City Books, 1994.

Niemeyer, Robert. A. (Ed.). *Meaning Reconstruction and the Experience of Loss*. Washington, DC: APA Press, 2003.

Oliver, Mary. "In Blackwater Woods," In *American Primitive*. Boston: Back Bay Books, 1993.

Osherson, Sam. *Finding Our Fathers*. New York: Fawcett, 1986.

Umberson, Debra. *Death of a Parent: Transition to a New Adult Identity*. United Kingdom: Cambridge, 2000.

*Dr. David E. Mullen*

# ABOUT THE AUTHOR

Dr. David E. Mullen is a clinical psychologist, marriage and family therapist, motivational speaker, and college professor. He is a positive psychologist who has spent over twenty five years helping individuals live fuller and more satisfying lives.

His first book was *Living Your Strengths: A Positive Psychology Approach*. The book is an introduction to this important area of contemporary psychology. A speaker at national and international workshops, *I Did Not Cry for My Father* is his second book. He has written articles for secular and professional journals. A seasoned psychotherapist, he has worked as director of an ecumenical counseling center, college counseling center and a staff psychologist at a community mental health center.

When he's not working, he is honing his skills as a jazz musician and putting together musical groups to raise money for local charities.

He is in the private practice of individual and couple psychotherapy in Sarasota, Florida. Please visit him at www.drdavidemullen.com.